DATE DUE

SEP 2 5 2004		2003
NOV 2 2 2004		
APR 2 2005		13
MAY 3 1 2005		B
SEP 1 3 2005		
NOV 2 9 '05		04
JUL 8 2006		2004
AUG 1 4 2006		202
FEB 7 2007		
MAR 2 2 2007		

MONSTERS
OF THE SEA

MONSTERS
OF THE SEA

by RITA GOLDEN GELMAN

Illustrated by JEAN DAY ZALLINGER

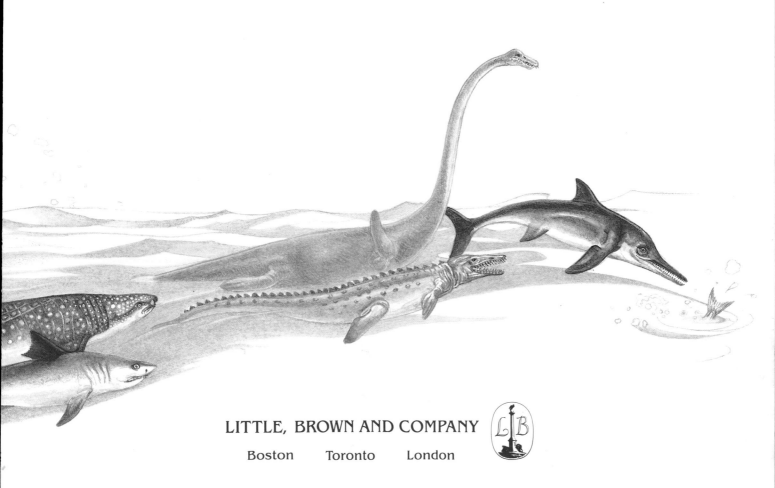

LITTLE, BROWN AND COMPANY

Boston   Toronto   London

To Samuel Franz David

J.D.Z.

Text copyright © 1990 by Rita Golden Gelman

Illustrations copyright © 1990 by Jean Day Zallinger

First edition

Library of Congress Cataloging-in-Publication Data

Gelman, Rita Golden.
    Monsters of the sea/by Rita Golden Gelman;
illustrated by Jean Day Zallinger.
        p.   cm.
    Summary: Illustrations and brief text depict twelve giant sea
creatures, some prehistoric and some modern.
    ISBN 0-316-30738-6
    1. Sea monsters — Juvenile literature. [1. Marine animals.
2. Sea monsters.] I. Zallinger, Jean, ill. II. Title.
QL89.2.S4G45 1990
591.92 — dc19   88-30794
                                                        CIP
                                                         AC

10   9   8   7   6   5   4   3   2   1
                        WOR

Published simultaneously in Canada
by Little, Brown & Company (Canada) Limited

Printed in the United States of America

Contents

Elasmosaurus 8

Ichthyosaur 10

Mosasaur 12

Great White Shark 14

Whale Shark 16

Giant Jellyfish 18

Manta Ray and Sawfish 20

Blue Whale 22

Killer Whale 24

Moray Eel 26

Giant Squid 28

Octopus 30

The Unknown 32

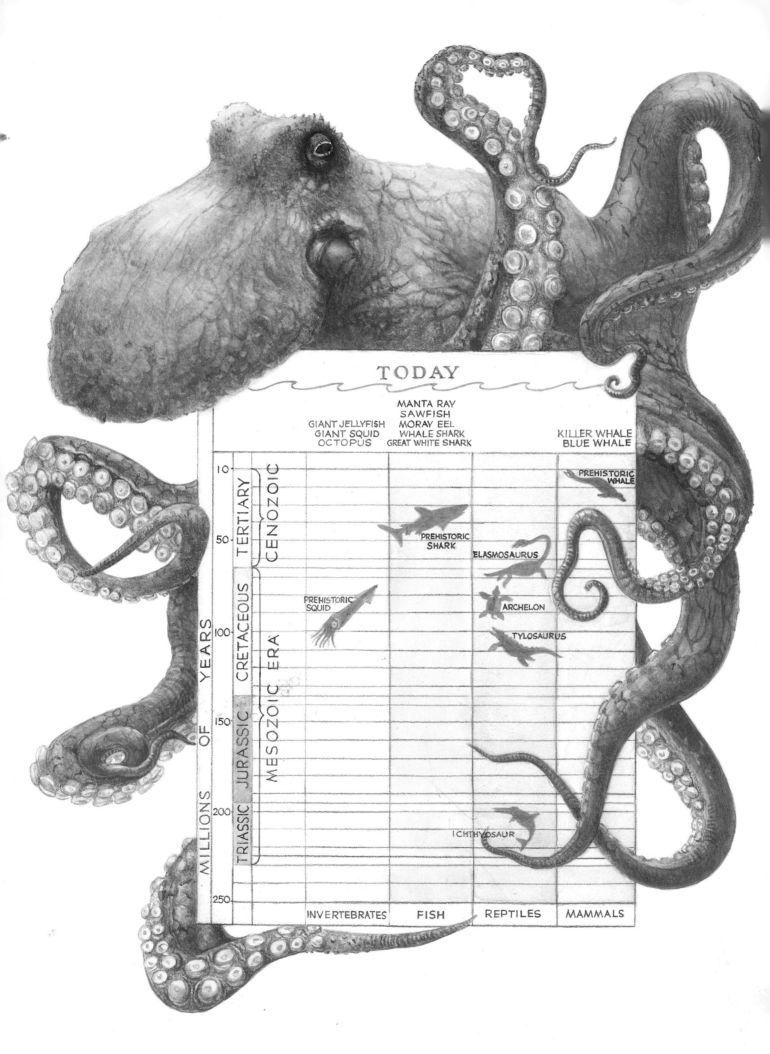

TODAY

MANTA RAY
SAWFISH
GIANT JELLYFISH   MORAY EEL
GIANT SQUID   WHALE SHARK   KILLER WHALE
OCTOPUS   GREAT WHITE SHARK   BLUE WHALE

MILLIONS OF YEARS			INVERTEBRATES	FISH	REPTILES	MAMMALS
10	TERTIARY	CENOZOIC				PREHISTORIC WHALE
50				PREHISTORIC SHARK	ELASMOSAURUS	
100	CRETACEOUS	MESOZOIC ERA	PREHISTORIC SQUID		ARCHELON TYLOSAURUS	
150	JURASSIC					
200	TRIASSIC				ICHTHYOSAUR	
250			INVERTEBRATES	FISH	REPTILES	MAMMALS

This is a book about monsters of the sea. Some are monsters because they are huge. Some are monsters because they are fierce. And some are monsters because they are very strange.

The first three monsters in the book lived and died millions of years ago. No person ever saw them.

The other monsters in the book are alive and well and still swimming.

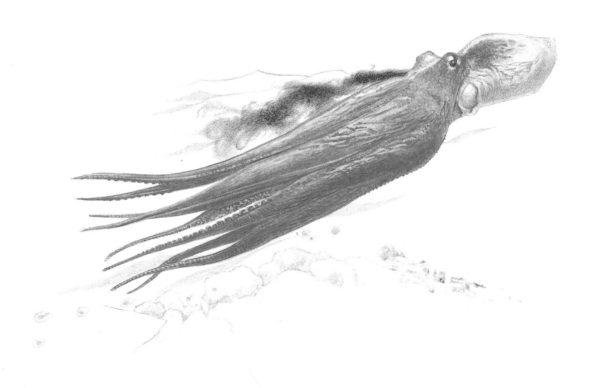

Elasmosaurus

(ee-*laz*-muh-*saw*-rus)

The elasmosaurus was a giant reptile that lived in all parts of the earth more than 200 million years ago. The elasmosaurus had a squat fat body, a short tail, and a long, long neck. From tail to head, it was about forty feet long.

The elasmosaurus also had four powerful fins. It used its fins like paddles to move forward. When it was tired of going forward, it paddled its fins the other way and went backward. And when it wanted to turn, it could move two fins forward and two backward, spinning itself around.

The elasmosaurus's neck was more than twice the length of a giraffe's neck. It used its long neck for catching meals of fish and small reptiles. Its mouth was full of long, jagged teeth that stuck out even when its jaws were closed!

Ichthyosaur

(*ik*-thee-uh-*sawr*)

Ichthyosaurs lived 185 million years ago, long before there were people on the earth. Ichthyosaurs were lizards that had fish fins instead of legs. They lived in the water, but they had to come up to the surface to breathe. Ichthyosaur means "fish-lizard."

Some ichthyosaurs were nearly forty feet long. Most were ten to thirty feet. They had pointy jaws with hundreds of sharp teeth. One ichthyosaur skeleton had a jaw that was seven feet long.

Ichthyosaurs were fast swimmers. They had streamlined bodies like porpoises, and they moved through the water by bending from side to side. They also had powerful tail fins that helped move them forward. But their leg fins were weak. Those were probably used for steering and braking. The fin on the ichthyosaur's back kept it from rolling over.

Ichthyosaurs probably ate anything they could get their teeth into. Good thing there were no people around!

Mosasaur

(*mo*-zuh-sawr)

The mosasaur lived in the water, but it wasn't a fish. It looked like a crocodile — but it wasn't that either. It was snakelike, but it wasn't a snake.

The mosasaur was a reptile with a long, thin body and a flat tail. Usually mosasaurs were twenty to twenty-six feet long. Some mosasaurs may have been forty feet long. They swam by wiggling their tails from side to side like crocodiles.

Mosasaurs lived seventy million years ago in the days of the dinosaurs. Most of the time they probably ate fish and turtles and other things that swam in the water. But mosasaurs, like snakes, could open their jaws very, very wide. Sometimes they might even have eaten small dinosaurs.

Great White Shark

Sharks also lived in the days of the dinosaurs. Their relatives are still swimming today in all the oceans of the world.

Great white sharks are usually ten to twenty feet long, but some are as big as forty feet. And they can weigh as much as six thousand pounds.

The great white shark has been called a "tooth machine." It has five or six rows of razor-sharp, jagged teeth. Some of the teeth are three inches long. When one of the front teeth falls out, a tooth from the next row pops up and moves forward within twenty-four hours. Even the shark's skin is covered with thousands of tiny teeth; shark skin feels like sandpaper.

The great white shark can crunch the steel propeller of a boat. Its jaws are the most powerful jaws in the world.

The great white shark will eat just about anything: squids, whales, turtles, seals. It will even eat horses and elephants that wade in shallow water. Sometimes the great white shark attacks people, too.

Sharks like to follow ships. They eat the garbage that is thrown overboard. Some of the things that have been found in shark stomachs are milk cartons, a woman's shoe, a telephone book, and a license plate.

Whale Shark

The whale shark is the biggest fish in the ocean. Some whale sharks grow to be sixty feet long — bigger than two school buses end to end. A whale shark's egg is bigger than a giant watermelon.

Whale sharks live in places where the water is warm, and they travel in herds. Groups of them swim slowly near the top of the water, sucking small fish and plants into their six-foot-wide mouths. Sometimes whale sharks "stand up" in the water, with their heads up and their tails down, to feed.

Unlike their cousins the great white sharks, whale sharks have tiny teeth, and they are no danger to people. Some whale sharks even give people rides on their backs.

Like all sharks, the whale shark has no bones. Instead, its skeleton is made of cartilage, the same kind of soft material that our ears are made of.

The whale shark has to keep moving to breathe. All fish breathe through gills, little slits on their bodies. Most fish have a flap to push water through their gills. Sharks have no flap. The only way sharks can get water through their gills is by swimming. They swim even while they sleep!

Giant Jellyfish

Giant jellyfish are soft and mushy because they have no bones. Their bodies look like huge, seven-foot-wide umbrellas. The biggest jellyfish live in the cold waters of the Arctic Ocean.

Some giant jellyfish are blue and look like big blobs of blueberry jelly. Some are orange and look like huge fried eggs.

Giant jellyfish seem beautiful when they float on top of the water. They also seem harmless since they have no sharp teeth,

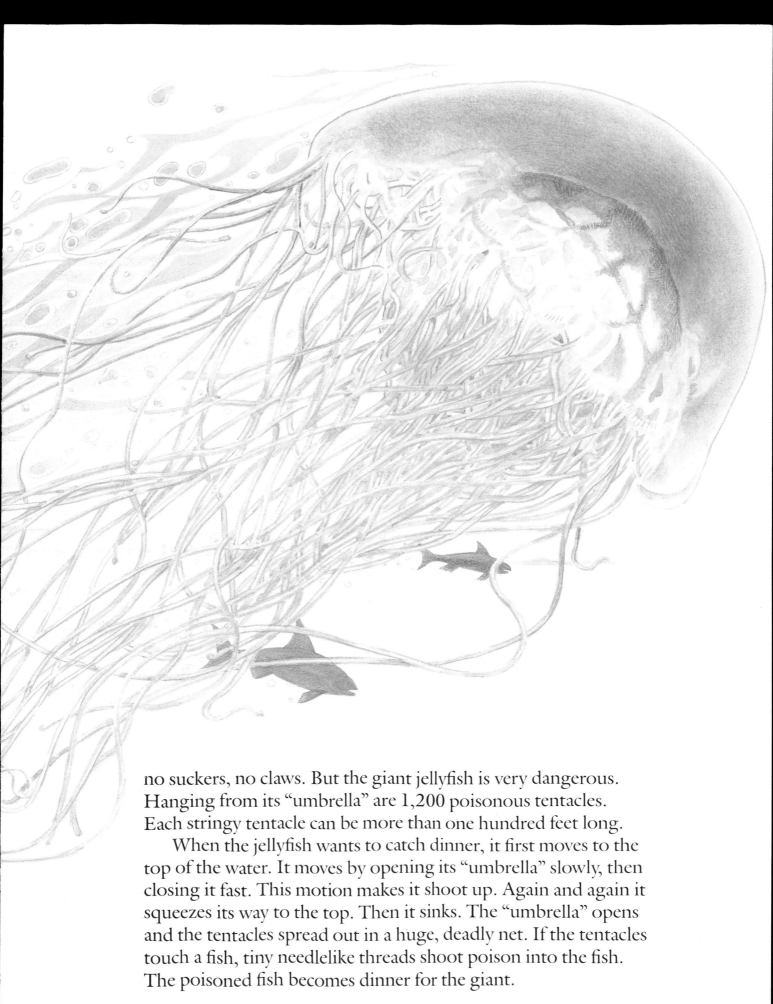

no suckers, no claws. But the giant jellyfish is very dangerous. Hanging from its "umbrella" are 1,200 poisonous tentacles. Each stringy tentacle can be more than one hundred feet long.

When the jellyfish wants to catch dinner, it first moves to the top of the water. It moves by opening its "umbrella" slowly, then closing it fast. This motion makes it shoot up. Again and again it squeezes its way to the top. Then it sinks. The "umbrella" opens and the tentacles spread out in a huge, deadly net. If the tentacles touch a fish, tiny needlelike threads shoot poison into the fish. The poisoned fish becomes dinner for the giant.

Manta Ray and Sawfish

Manta rays have been around for millions of years, swimming in warm-water seas. The manta ray weighs between three and four thousand pounds, and when it's all spread out, it can stretch to twenty-two feet. It looks like a giant kite.

The manta can even fly like a kite. It leaps out of the water and soars through the air, as high as fifteen feet above the water. When the manta comes down, it hits with a giant bellyflop. When a whole school of flying mantas hits the water, the noise is like thunder!

When it is hungry, the manta opens its giant mouth and swims through a school of small fish, collecting dinner as it swims.

The manta has two large fins that stick out from its head. The fins look like horns. That's why the manta is sometimes called "the devil fish."

The sawfish ray is a cousin of the manta, but unlike the manta, it has a long and narrow body and a swordlike snout with sharp dagger teeth along the sides. Sawfish can be up to twenty feet long, with six-foot-long saws.

The sawfish can kill many fish at once by swinging its saw from side to side. Little fish are speared and the big ones are sliced in half.

Blue Whale

The blue whale is the largest animal that ever lived. It is bigger than the biggest dinosaur and heavier than 2,000 people. Blue whales can weigh more than 300,000 pounds and be more than eighty feet long.

Whales swim in oceans all over the world, but they are not fish; they are mammals. Whale babies are born live, and they drink milk from their mothers.

A newborn blue whale is as big as a bus. It weighs six thousand pounds. And it grows fast! A nursing baby can gain as much as two hundred pounds a day.

Whales can't breathe under the water the way fish can; a whale has to hold its breath when it dives. Some whales can stay under · water for an hour. Others have to come up after five minutes.

When the whale comes up, it breathes out through a blow-hole. This moist, warm air turns into steam and becomes the whale's spout. Some whales spout as high as twenty feet.

The blue whale has no teeth. Instead, it has strainers called baleen. As the blue whale swims along, it fills its mouth and enormous throat with water. Then the whale closes its mouth and empties the water through the strainers. Tiny plants and animals are trapped inside. And that's how the blue whale gets food.

Killer Whales

Killer whales are about thirty feet long and weigh around 16,000 pounds. They can be found in every ocean on the earth. Adult killer whales are black and white. The babies are black and bright orange.

The killer whale uses its large teeth to tear its prey apart. Killer whales feed mostly on fish, but they have been known to eat seals, polar bears, penguins, and walruses. They even attack other whales.

If you should happen to see a killer whale, you can tell if it's a male or female by looking at its back fins. A male's back fin is triangular; the female's is shaped like a crescent moon.

Even though they are called whales, killer whales are actually porpoises. Like all porpoises, killer whales are very intelligent. Most animals have brains that are smooth on the outside. Porpoise brains are crinkled — just like human brains.

Killer whales move in groups. The females (called cows) stay with the children (calves) in the middle of the group, and

the males (bulls) surround them as they swim along. Sometimes the lead male is way ahead of the group. When he wants to signal the others to change direction, he slaps the water with his side fins, or he jumps up and slams his body back into the water. The sound of his splash can be heard six miles away.

Scientists think that the leaders may send voice signals as well. Like other porpoises, killer whales make noises in the water. Sometimes the killer whale oinks like a pig. Sometimes it barks like a dog. And sometimes the killer whale whistles.

Moray Eel

Moray eels look like long, fat snakes. But they are really fish that live on the ocean bottom. They squiggle their five-to-eleven-foot-long bodies around in the mud, and they swim in and out of the coral reefs in warm, tropical, and subtropical waters.

Octopuses also live on the bottom of the ocean and in coral reefs. Morays and octopuses are enemies. The octopus looks scarier than the moray, but morays have deadly teeth that can bite through the octopus's skin. Morays eat octopuses.

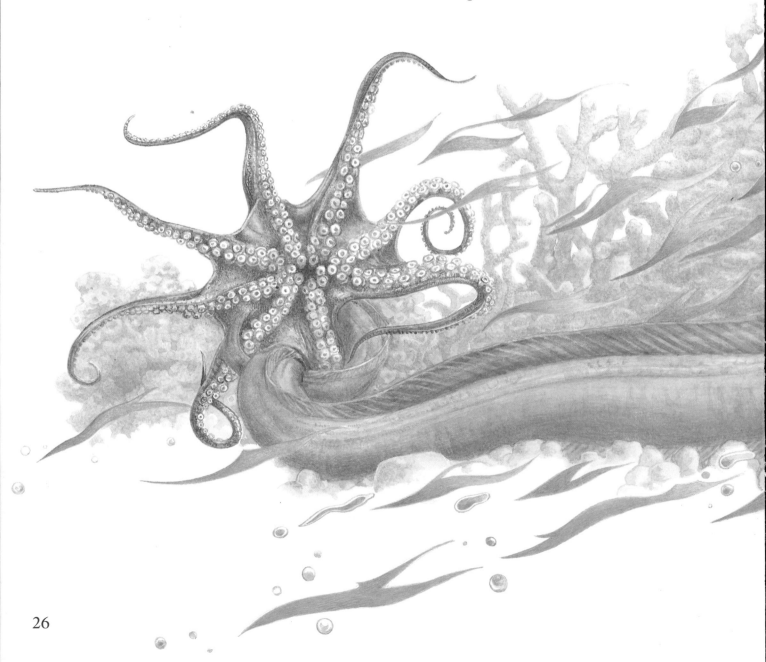

Sometimes the octopus clamps its suckers onto the moray. The moray has a trick to get the octopus off. The moray ties its tail into a knot. The hole in the knot is just big enough for the moray to go through headfirst. The moray's skin is slippery. As the moray squeezes its long body through the hole, the octopus slips off.

Giant Squid

Squids come in all sizes. Some are tiny. Some are huge.

The giant squid is the largest of all. Scientists think that some giant squids may have bodies as big as fifty feet across and arms that are thirty-five feet long. The giant squid's eyes are fifteen inches wide. They are the biggest eyes in the world.

Squids have eight arms with sucking disks all along them. They also have two tentacles, even longer than the arms. The tentacles reach out and grab fish, pulling them in until the squid's arms can grasp them tight — and serve them for dinner!

The squid is a super swimmer. And it doesn't even use its arms. It usually swims along slowly, but when it wants to go fast, the squid sucks water into its body and shoots it out through a hose. A squid can point its hose in any direction and jet wherever it wants to go.

The giant squid lives in the deepest parts of the North Atlantic Ocean . . . and probably in all the oceans of the earth. But no one knows for sure because people can't go down that deep, and squids don't come up. Almost everything we know about giant squids is from remains that have washed up on beaches or from the contents of the sperm whale's stomach.

Octopus

The octopus is a cousin of the squid. The octopus has a jet hose, too. But it uses its hose only for emergencies. Most of the time the octopus crawls along the bottom of the ocean, wherever the water is warm.

Octopuses can be small, medium, or large. The largest ones measure about thirty feet from the tip of one tentacle to the tip of the opposite one.

The octopus crawls on its eight armlike tentacles. On the bottom side of each arm are two long rows of suckers.

The octopus uses its suckers to hold on to slippery rocks and to catch dinner. Octopuses love to eat crabs. The octopus hides in the rocks and waits for a crab to come along, then it reaches out with an arm and clamps the crab onto one of the suckers. One diver saw an octopus holding on to seventeen crabs at once.

The octopus has a special ink trick. If one of its enemies comes too close, it squirts out a blob of ink. The enemy thinks the blob is the octopus. By the time the enemy realizes its mistake, the octopus has escaped. Squids use the same trick. Octopus ink is black. Squid ink is brown.

Octopuses and squids have another trick that is even better. They can change their color. They can turn themselves brown or white or red or orange. Or dark or light. They can even make themselves spotted or striped. The octopus and squid can go from one color to another in less than one second.

The Unknown

Those are just some of the monsters we know about.

There could be monsters on the bottom of the ocean that no one has ever seen. Maybe, hiding deep in unexplored waters, there are creatures even bigger than the blue whale, more dangerous than the great white shark, and stranger than the elasmosaurus.

Maybe we'll discover them someday. Or maybe we won't!